SHINY X-MAS

HELLA HENCKEL

DAS GROSSE BUCH DER WEIHNACHTSFLORISTIK – THE ULTIMATE COLLECTION

BLOOM's PROFESSIONAL

HERAUSGEBER PUBLISHER
BLOOM's GmbH, Ratingen (D)

REDAKTION & TEXT EDITOR & TEXT
Hella Henckel

FLORISTIK FLORAL DESIGN
Vom BLOOM's-Team außer: By BLOOM's-Team exept:
Julia Isabelle Bürkle: 158–159 * Maike Bußmann: 032, 033 oben above * Jürgen Herold: 045 * Björn Kroner-Salié: 105–111, 200–203 * Manuela Ostertag: 029, 081–082, 085 rechts right, 086–089, 093–099, 145–147 oben above, 148–157, 232–233 * Ilka Siedenburg: 184–185, 191

GRAFIKDESIGN GRAPHIC DESIGN
Marion Hennig

DTP DTP
Britta Baschen

FOTOS PHOTOGRAPHY
Patrick Pantze Images GmbH, Lage (D), außer exept:
Hintergrund Background: colors0613 - Fotolia.com * Cover, 001, 003, 005, 006, 030, 046, 078, 102, 160, 182, 210: kolotuschenko - Fotolia.com * 006: sasel77 - Fotolia.com * 046: dianamower - Fotolia.com * 062: by-studio - Fotolia.com * 072: Light Impression - Fotolia.com * 132: haru - Fotolia.com * 160: Stefan Balk - Fotolia.com * 164: Carola Schubbel - Fotolia.com * 210: Rick Sargeant - Fotolia.com * 236: natu - Shutterstock

ÜBERSETZUNG TRANSLATION
Janet Brümmer, Beyond Words, Düsseldorf (D)

DRUCK PRINT
Westermann Druck GmbH, Zwickau (D)

Am Potekamp 6 * D-40885 Ratingen
T +49 2102 9644-0 * F +49 2102 896073
info@blooms.de * www.blooms.de

1. AUFLAGE 2016 1ST EDITION 2016

ISBN 978-3-945429-60-0

www.blooms.de

INHALT
CONTENTS

VORWORT
FOREWORD

GLANZVOLLES WEIHNACHTEN! Einmal im Jahr ist alles ganz anders! Wenn das Weihnachtsfest naht, soll es überall festlich sein! Dann werden nicht nur der Tisch oder die Fensterbänke geschmückt, sondern ganze Räume mit weihnachtlichem Glanz überzogen. Auch wer sich das Jahr über eher als Purist präsentiert, genießt nun dekorative Gemütlichkeit, lässt mit dem Kerzenschein die weihnachtliche Stimmung aufkommen und schwelgt in Tradition und Erinnerungsgefühlen. In diesem Buch haben wir Ihnen eine Fülle recht unterschiedlicher Ideen zusammengestellt, die für jeden Geschmack, für jede Anforderung und für jede Situation das Passende bietet. Ob Adventskranz oder Weihnachtsbaum, vom Tischgesteck bis zur Treppengirlande, ob kleines, adventliches Mitbringsel oder opulenter weihnachtlicher Feststrauß: Sie finden liebevoll Gestaltetes, dass die Weihnachtszeit bezaubernd macht!
Viel Freude mit den besten weihnachtlichen Dekorationsideen vom BLOOM's-Team der letzten Jahre!

SHINY CHRISTMAS! Once a year the world becomes a different place! As the Christmas celebration draws near, we want everything to be festive! Now is the time to not only adorn the table and windowsills, but to also fill entire rooms with a Christmas glow. Even for those who prefer a more purist style the rest of the year can enjoy the decorative cosiness of this time, creating a Christmas atmosphere with the glow of candlelight while basking in the traditions and memories of Christmases past. In this book we have compiled a vast collection of all kinds of ideas, with solutions to suit every preference, meet every requirement and fit every situation. Whether an Advent wreath or a Christmas tree, from table arrangements to garlands for a railing, be it a small present for a host or hostess or an opulent Christmas bouquet – here you will find lots of lovingly created designs, which will make your Christmas a captivating season! We hope you have fun with the best Christmas decoration ideas from the BLOOM's team over the past few years!

Die FESTLICHKEIT der NATURTÖNE

Die Natur mit ihren reichhaltigen Schätzen bestimmt auch winterlich-weihnachtliche Dekorationsideen. Zapfen, raues Holz, Rinde, trockene Gräser, Zweige oder Flechten punkten mit ihrer ganz eigenen Schönheit. Natürlichkeit ist „in“!

FESTIVITY IN NATURAL SHADES Mother Nature with her treasure trove of materials also provides the inspiration for wintry Christmas decoration ideas. Cones, rough wood, bark, dried grasses, branches and lichen score points with their own brand of natural beauty. Nature is “in”!

NATURLIEBE
NATURAL IDYL

Das FRISCHE von PETROL

Rhapsodie in mutiger Farbgebung. Gezielte Akzente geben jeder Zusammenstellung die moderne Frische. Ob Großstadtnomaden oder Traditionsverliebte, hier wird weihnachtlicher Glanz ganz neu interpretiert.

PATINA OF PETROL A rhapsody in daring colours. Well-placed accents give every composition a touch of modern freshness. City nomads and traditionalists alike will appreciate this new interpretation of Christmas shine.

Das WOHLGEFÜHL von ROT

Kaum eine Farbe vermittelt mehr das weihnachtliche Gefühl von Wärme und sehnsuchtsvoller Erinnerung an kindliche Geborgenheit als das festliche Rot. Natürlich-rustikal interpretiert und immer mit traditioneller Rückbesinnung spricht Floristik in diesem Stil nicht nur Romantiker an.

RADIANCE OF RED Hardly any other colour conveys the Christmas feeling of warmth and the fond memories of a carefree childhood as festive red. In a natural and rustic interpretation and always with a return to old traditions, floristry in this style appeals not only to romantic souls.

BEDEUTSAMKEIT
MEANINGFUL

HERZENSWÄRME
WARMHEARTED

Die VIELFALT von GOLD

Transparentes Design liebt glänzende Highlights. Ob prächtiges Gold bei Kerzen und Accessoires oder Lichterketten in Gestecken oder Sträußen – dieser sinnliche Überschwang lässt ein modernes Märchen wahrwerden, auch für Metropoliten.

GLEAM OF GOLD Transparent designs love radiant highlights. Whether it's lustrous gold in the candles and accessories or fairy lights glowing inside arrangements or bouquets – this sensual exuberance gives life to a modern fairy tale, even for metropolitans.

GLANZZEITEN
GLORIOUS

Das BELEBENDE von TÜRKIS

Nirgends werden Widersprüche beeindruckender zelebriert als im kindlichen Umfeld. Neue Farbzusammenstellungen und ungewöhnliche Kombinationen sorgen für überraschende Momente voller Esprit und Lebensfreude: Sternstunden für Familienorientierte und Mutige!

TWINKLE OF TURQUOISE Nowhere are contrasts celebrated more exuberantly than where children are involved. New colour mixtures and unusual combinations guarantee surprising moments full of esprit and joie de vivre. Star performance for the family-oriented and courageous among us!

HEITERKEIT
HAPPINESS

Der CHARME der PASTELLE

Wenn die Poesie der Farben tonangebend ist, hat die sinnenfrohe Aura einen perfekten Auftritt. Die Dekorationsideen spielen mit femininer Geziertheit und formvollendeter Eleganz. Ein Comeback jenseits aller Moden aber mit dem Charme der Lieblichkeit.

PANACHE OF PASTELS When the poetry of colour sets the stage, the moment is perfect for a sensuous performance. The decoration ideas are an interplay of feminine grace and flawless elegance. A comeback beyond all fashion trends, but with the charm of true loveliness.

LIEBLICHKEIT
LOVELINESS

Das WÜRDEVOLLE von BRAUN

Erinnerungen an gediegene Lebensstile und Inseln der Behaglichkeit werden wach, wenn stolze Formen und klassische Zitate neue Designs bestimmen. Kerzenleuchter strahlen würdevolle Ruhe aus, Objekte zeigen sich charaktervoll und detailreich und die floralen Objekte erinnern an mondäne Zeiten voller Komfort und Anspruch.

BRILLIANCE OF BROWN Memories of elegant lifestyles and cosy oases of wellbeing are awakened when proud shapes and classic quotes determine the new designs. Candle holders radiate a dignified calm, objects show character and fine details while the floral arrangements are redolent of glamorous times full of comfort and sophistication.

CHARAKTERVOLL
CHARACTERFUL

.. Das FRÖHLICHE der BUNTHEIT

Wer ein Fest im Rausch der Farben inszeniert, gibt dem Leben neue Power. Eine bunte Heiterkeit prägt den unkonventionellen Stil, in dem dekorative Fülle gewünscht und Zurückhaltung fehl am Platze ist. Szene-People und modische Trendsetter werden Weihnachten in diesem Farbfeuer lieben.

HIGHLIGHTS OF HUES When you stage festivities awash in colour, the decorations lend new power to your life. A bright and colourful world characterizes the unconventional style in which decorative abundance is the preference and restraint has no place. Scene people and stylish trendsetters will love Christmas in this explosion of colour.

FARBENRAUSCH
COLOUR BLAZE

Die PRÄCHTIGKEIT von WEISS-SILBER

Winterliche Klarheit und gestalterische Leichtigkeit gehen eine neue Liaison ein, bei der eine einzige Farbe ihr konturenreiches Profil zeigt. Weiß weckt Gefühle und steigert die Lust auf winterlich inspirierte Dekoideen, die die Natur ins Haus holen. Der perfekte Style für Ästheten und zeitlose Klassiker.

SHIMMER OF SILVER Wintry clarity and lightness of design enter into a new liaison in which a single colour showcases her richly-contoured profile. Silvery-white awakens emotions and arouses a desire for deco ideas inspired by winter, which bring nature into our homes. The perfect style for aesthetes and lovers of timeless classics.

KRISTALLKLAR
CRYSTAL CLEAR